Introducing: An E-Z approach to playing the piano.

And E-Z really means easy! The E-Z Play® TODAY Piano Series was created for anyone and everyone who:

- wants to learn to play the piano
- doesn't have time to take music lessons
- wants to play popular songs and favorite tunes **instantly!**

BEGINNINGS 1 will show you the E-Z way to reading music. Each new music element is explained and illustrated, then applied to well-known melodies. You'll learn the E-Z approach to several fundamental accompaniment styles, too.

And, as a special feature, a Reference Guide for Supplementary Songs in this series is located in the back of this book. This guide lists dozens of songs which will add to your playing pleasure.

Once you've completed this book, you'll probably want to continue your learning adventure in BEGINNINGS 2 FOR PIANO. In this second volume, you'll be introduced to more advanced playing techniques and many more songs . . . all presented in this unique easy-to-play format.

E-Z PLAY is a registered trademark of HAL LEONARD PUBLISHING CORPORATION.

HAL•LEONARD CORPORATION
7777 W. BLUEMOUND RD. P.O. BOX 13819 MILWAUKEE, WI 53213

KEYBOARD GUIDE

To make it possible for you to easily learn the keys on your piano, a **keyboard guide** is included with this book. Place this guide on the keyboard as shown in the illustration on the inside front cover.

COLOR CODED LABELS

Color coded labels are also included to help you become instantly familiar with the bass and accompaniment sections of the keyboard. Attach these labels to the keyboard as shown in the illustration on the inside front cover.

MUSIC NOTATION

All songs are written in the exclusive E-Z Play TODAY Music Notation.

● A STAFF is five horizontal lines with spaces between the lines. Each line or space represents a specific note (key) on the piano.

● Sometimes LEDGER LINES are added above or below the staff to accommodate additional notes.

LEDGER LINES

LEDGER LINES

● The lettered notes correspond to lettered keys on the keyboard guide. As notes move down the staff, the corresponding keys move down (to the left) on the keyboard. As the notes move up the staff, they move up (to the right) on the keyboard.

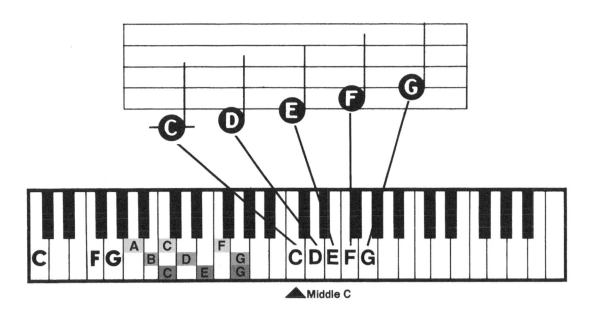

Middle C

● Each type of note has a specific TIME VALUE which is measured in rhythmic beats.

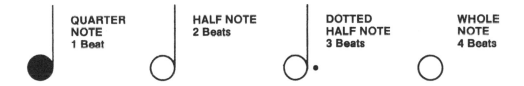

QUARTER NOTE
1 Beat

HALF NOTE
2 Beats

DOTTED HALF NOTE
3 Beats

WHOLE NOTE
4 Beats

● Each staff is divided by BAR LINES into sections called MEA-SURES. A DOUBLE BAR indicates the end of a song.

MEASURE   MEASURE

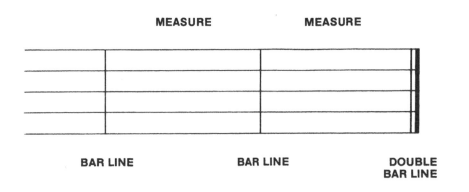

BAR LINE   BAR LINE   DOUBLE BAR LINE

- A TIME SIGNATURE appears at the beginning of each song after the TREBLE CLEF sign.

The **top number** indicates the number of rhythmic beats in each measure.

The **bottom number** indicates the type of note that receives one beat. 4 indicates a quarter note.

4 beats in each measure

A quarter note gets one beat

3 beats in each measure

A quarter note gets one beat

- A TIE is a curved line that connects notes of the same pitch (notes on the same line or space). Play the first note and then hold for the total time of all tied notes.

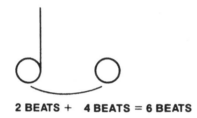

2 BEATS + 4 BEATS = 6 BEATS   4 BEATS + 4 BEATS = 8 BEATS

Play and count this example before going ahead.

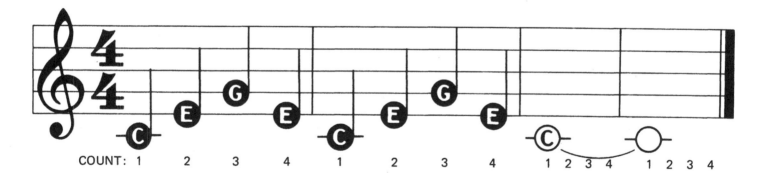

COUNT: 1   2   3   4   1   2   3   4   1 2 3 4   1 2 3 4

- Various playing techniques are important to learn from the very beginning. For example, to produce a smooth sounding melody, it is extremely important to play the keys using the proper fingering.

Fingering numbers will appear next to the melody notes like this:

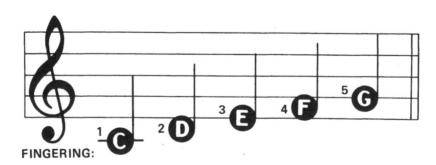

FINGERING:

These numbers correspond to your right-hand fingers like this:

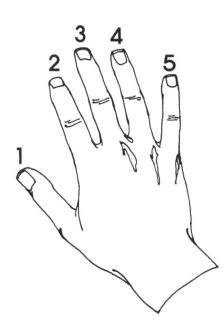

Here's the melody to the first song, MERRILY WE ROLL ALONG. Carefully read the notes and play the corresponding keys with your right hand.

Merrily We Roll Along

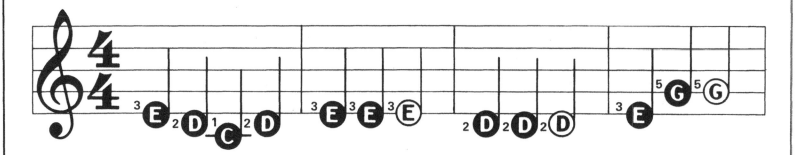

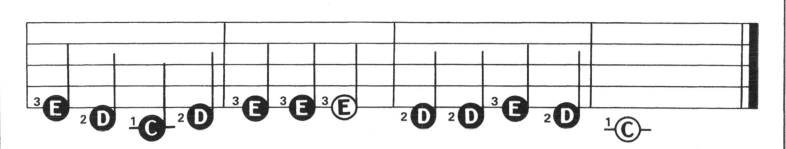

Accompaniment is the chord harmony which is played by your left hand. (Chords are combinations of three or more musical tones which are sounded simultaneously.)

In each E-Z Play TODAY arrangement, the accompaniment chords are indicated by boxed symbols which appear above the melody notes. These chord symbols indicate which chord to play.

CHORD SYMBOLS

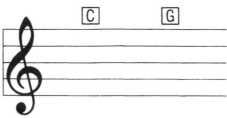

The C and G chords that you'll use in your first song are color-coded on your keyboard guide. The fingering numbers which appear for the chords in the keyboard illustrations correspond to your left-hand fingers like this:

Press the keys that are color coded **red** and you'll be playing a ⃞C chord.

▼ Middle C

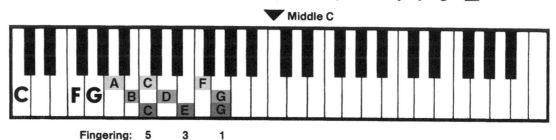

Fingering:　5　3　1

Press these keys for a ⃞C chord.

Press the keys that are color coded **green** and you'll be playing the ⃞G chord.

▼ Middle C

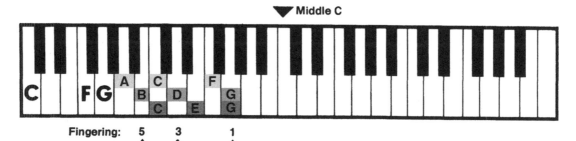

Fingering:　5　3　1

Press these keys for a ⃞G chord.

Practice changing back and forth from the C (red) chord to the G (green) chord until you can make the change smoothly.

Now, play the first two songs using both right-hand melody and left-hand accompaniment. Remember to:
1. Match the melody notes to the corresponding keys and play.
2. At the same time, play the left-hand chord accompaniment according to the indicated chord symbol. Be sure to hold each chord until the next chord symbol appears in the music.

Song 1: Merrily We Roll Along

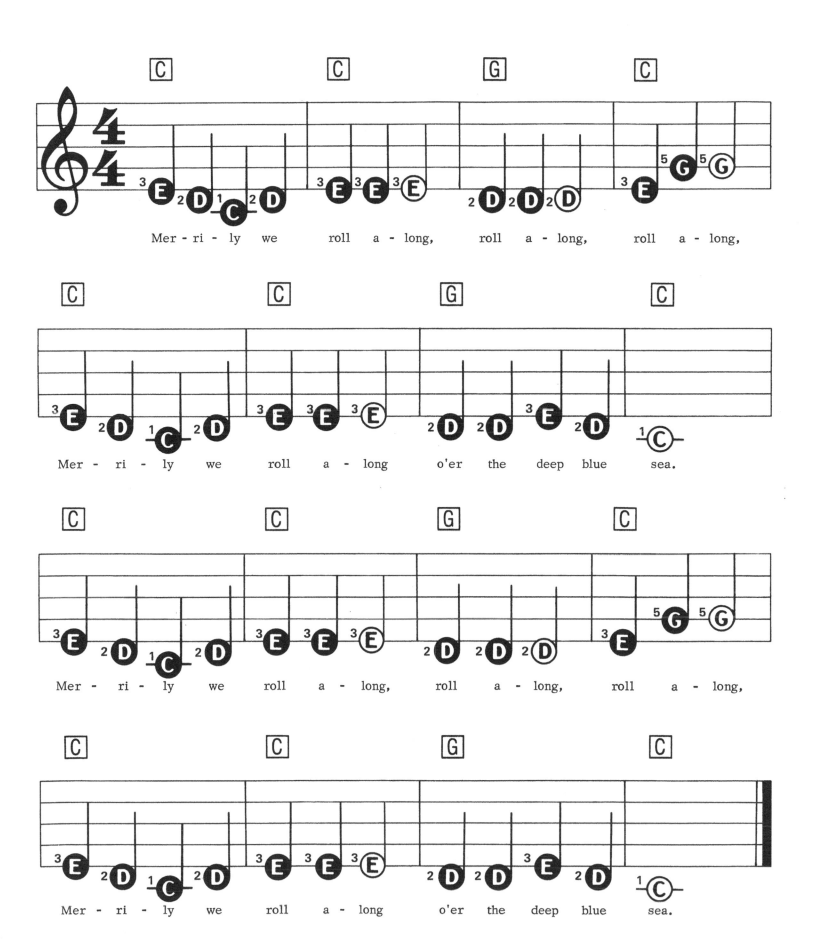

7

Song 2: Ode To Joy

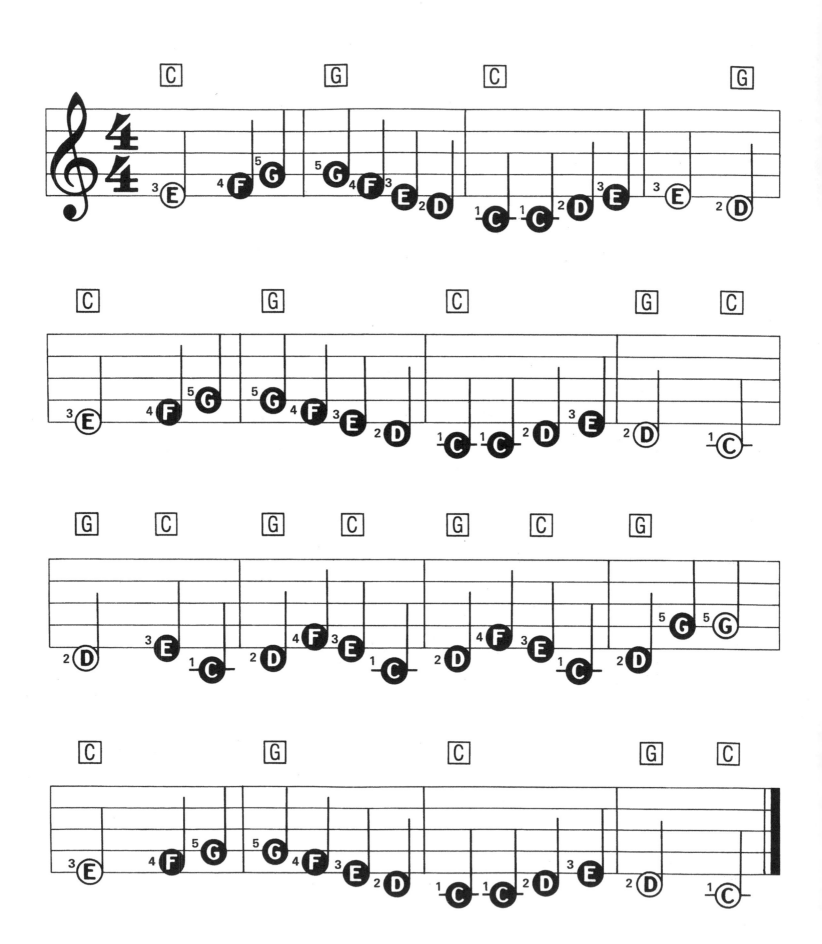

INTRODUCING A NEW CHORD ℉

Press the keys that are color coded **blue** and you'll be playing an ℉ chord.

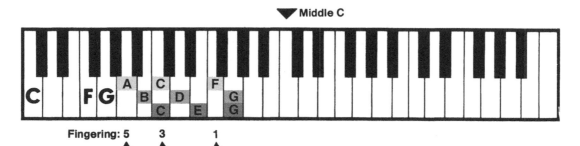

Fingering: 5   3   1

Press these keys for an ℉ chord.

PICK-UP NOTES

You read earlier that the top number of a time signature indicates the number of rhythmic beats in a measure. Frequently, the time value of the notes at the beginning of a song does not equal a full measure. These notes are called PICK-UP NOTES. The missing beats of that measure are usually found at the end of a song.

The following example illustrates **Pick-up** notes in your next song.

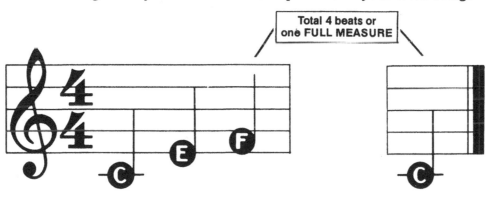

Total 4 beats or one FULL MEASURE

Pick-up notes in Song 3   Last measure of Song 3

N.C. SIGN

N.C. is an abbreviation for NO CHORD. When N.C. appears above the staff, it means that no chord is played . . . just the right-hand melody.

Song 3: When The Saints Go Marching In

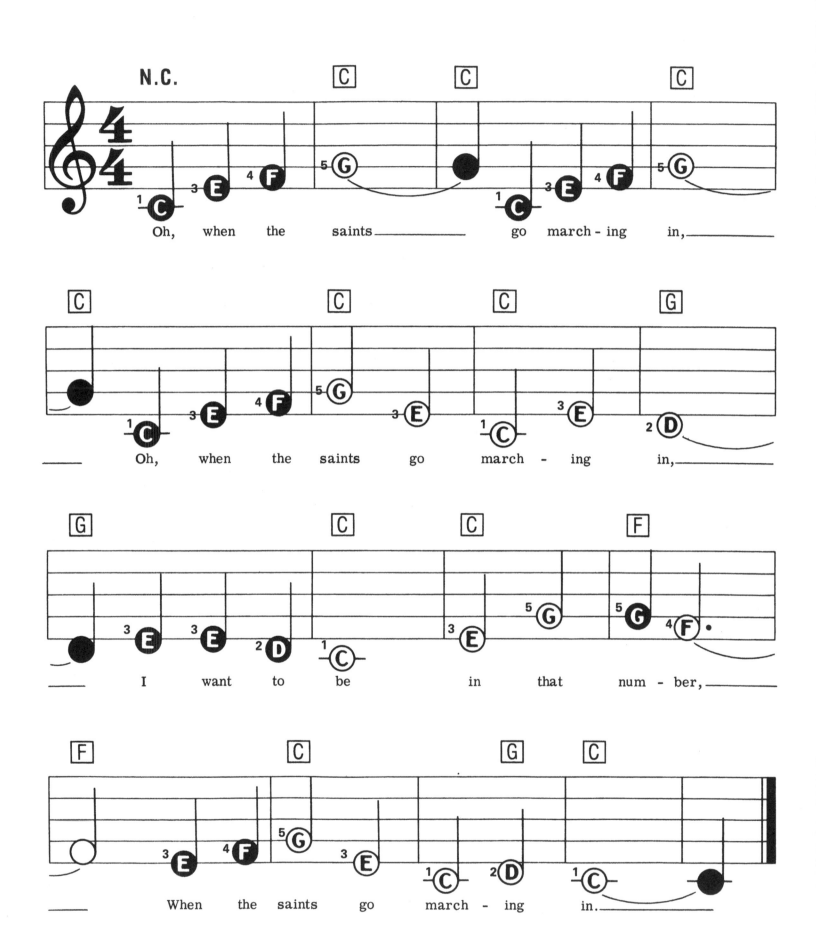

Song 4: Beautiful Brown Eyes

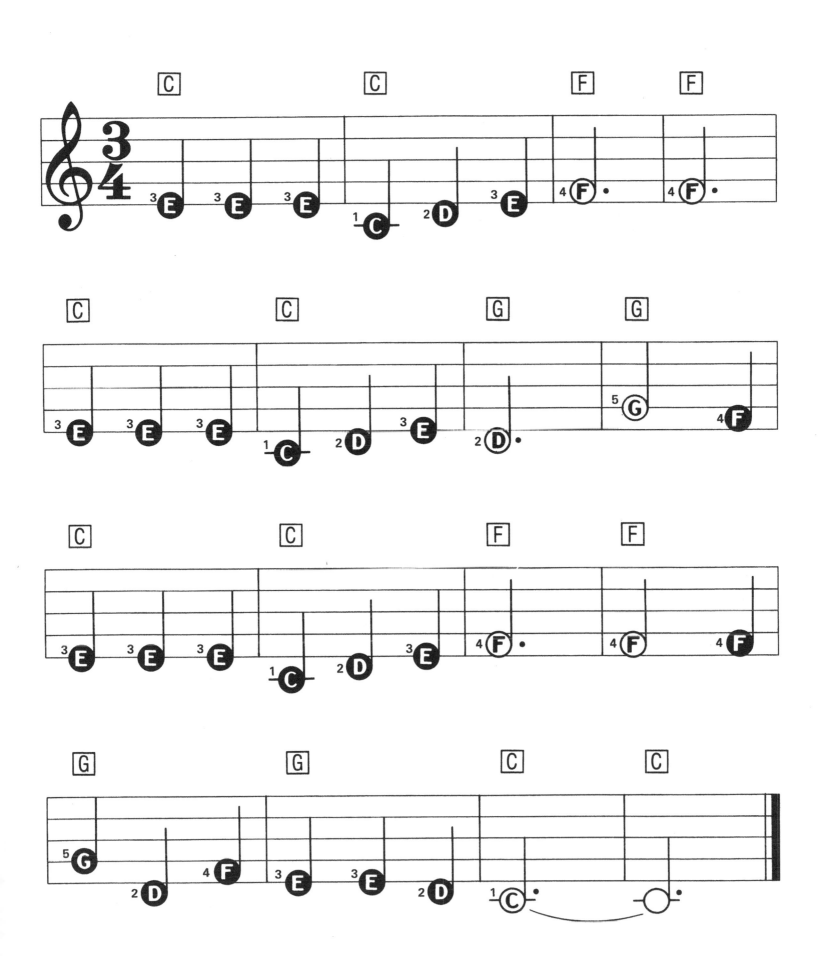

Thus far, the left-hand accompaniment has consisted entirely of chords. These chords have been indicated on the music by a boxed letter; Ⓒ, Ⓕ, Ⓖ. Starting with the next arrangement, you'll also use single notes in the accompaniment. These single notes are indicated by the letters which appear above the staff. **The letters which indicate single notes do not have a box around them.** To play single notes, merely match the unboxed letters with the same letters which you'll find on your keyboard guide and play. (You have already placed accompaniment keyboard labels for the C, F and G notes on the left end of the piano keyboard.)

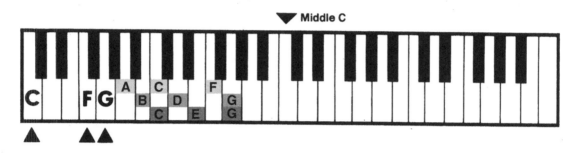

This is the area of the keyboard where single notes C, F and G are played.

Try the following exercise before going on. Use the 5th (little) finger of your left hand to play all the single notes and the same fingering you already know to play the chords.

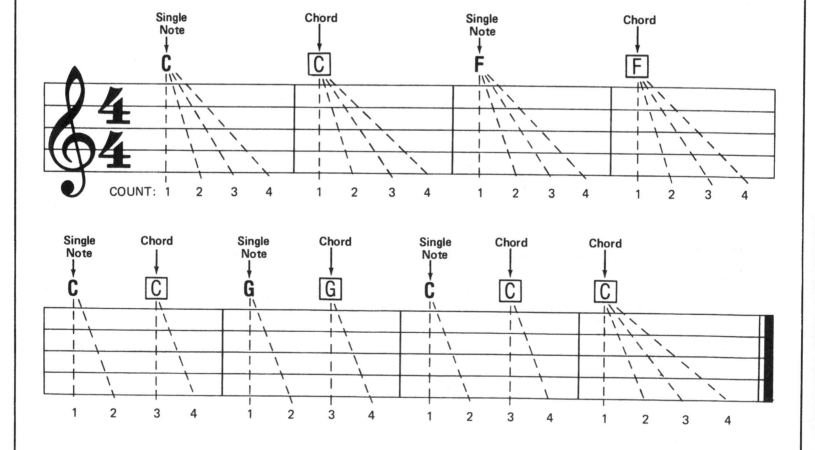

In the next song, there is a new melody note . . . B. In this song, it's played with the first finger of the right hand.

● It appears like this on the staff.

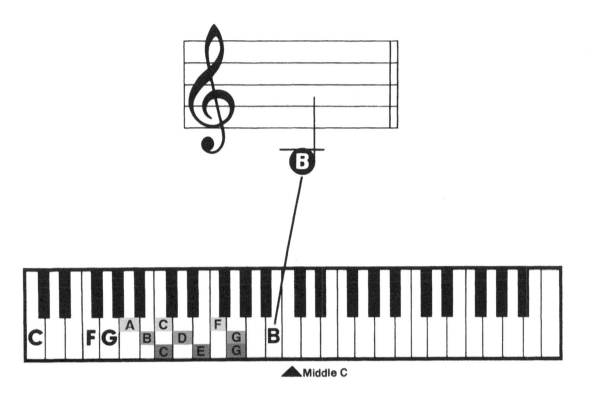

● It corresponds to this key on the keyboard.

NOTE: From this point on, you will be using **more** than five melody notes in a song. Therefore, it is more important than ever to observe the fingering. Remember, the number which appears next to a melody note in the music indicates which finger to use to play that key on the piano.

Song 5: Marianne

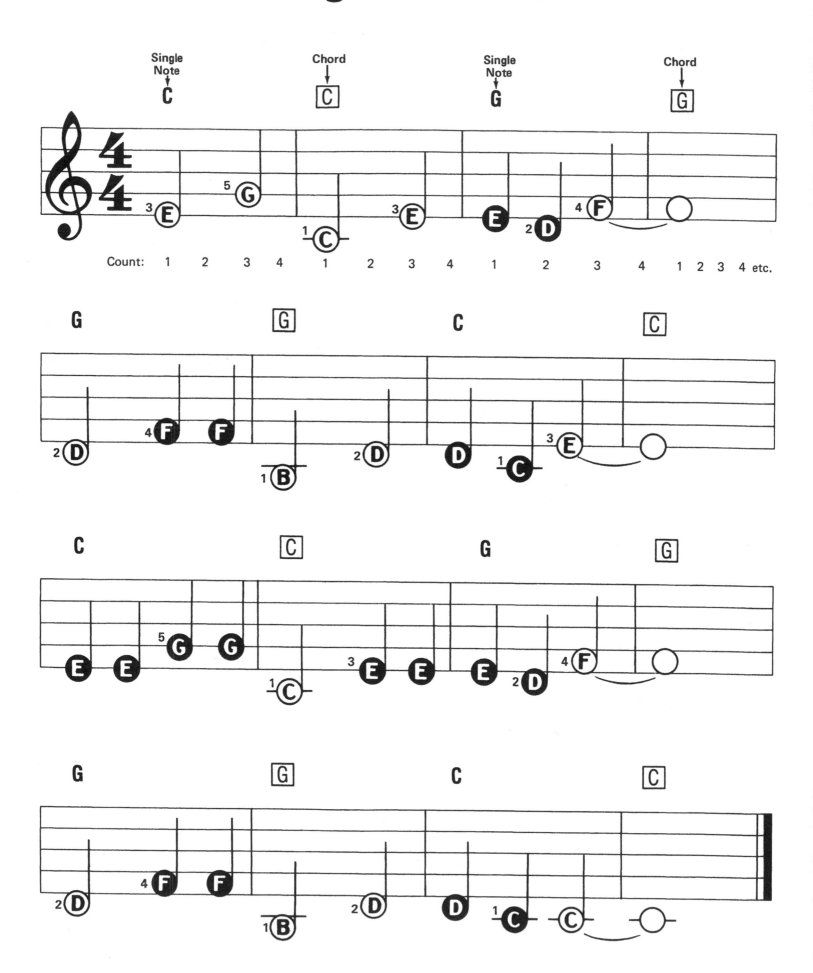

Song 6 contains the new melody note A. In this song, the A note is played with the 5th (little) finger of your right hand.

● It appears like this on the staff.

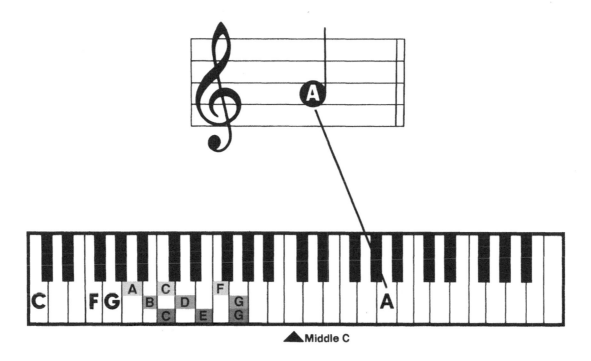

● It corresponds to this key on the keyboard.

Song 6: Michael, Row The Boat Ashore

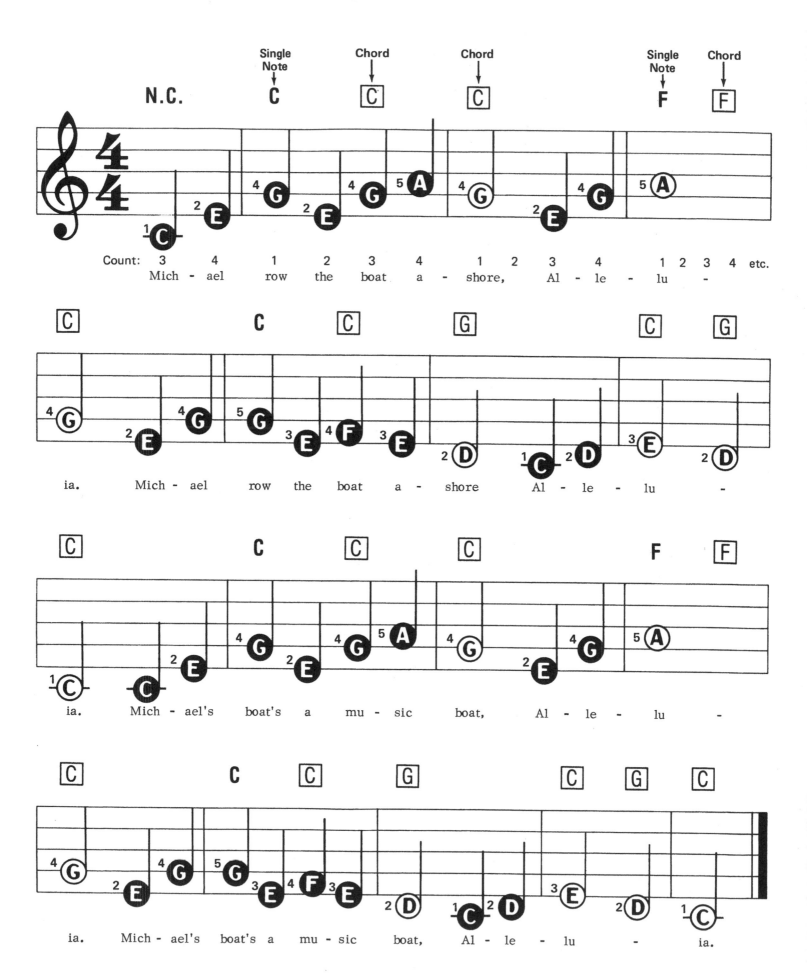

THE SUSTAIN PEDAL

▲ SUSTAIN PEDAL

At the base of the piano, you'll find a set of either two or three pedals.

The pedal that's farthest to the right is called the **Sustain Pedal.**

When you press and hold this pedal with your foot and play a key or keys on the piano, the tones continue to sound (sustain) long after your fingers are removed from the keyboard. The Sustain Pedal helps to create a "fullness" of sound which adds smoothness and continuity to your playing.

When the Sustain Pedal is to be used, you'll see the symbol *Ped* marked below the music staff. Continue to hold this pedal until you see either another *Ped* (in which case you release the pedal and immediately press and hold it again) or the symbol *RPed* (meaning release pedal).

INTRODUCING A NEW CHORD . . . G7

Press these keys and you'll be playing a G7 chord. Be sure to watch the new fingering.

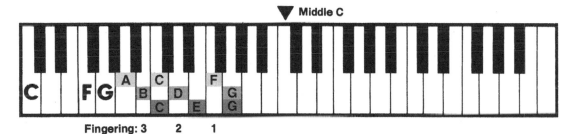

▼ Middle C

Fingering: 3   2   1

Press these keys for a G7 chord.

INTRODUCING RESTS

Rests are symbols which indicate periods of silence. They correspond to the time values of notes having the same name.

QUARTER REST
1 Beat of silence

HALF REST
2 Beats of silence

WHOLE REST
4 Beats of silence

Song 7: Kumbaya

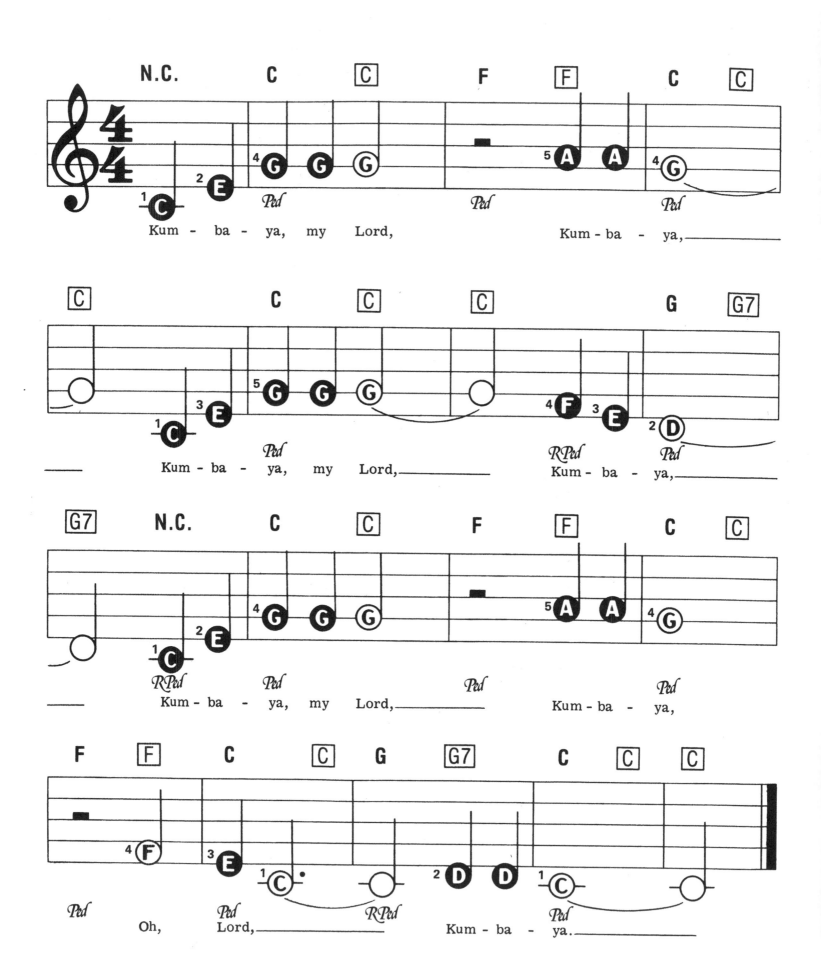

INTRODUCING HALF-STEPS

A HALF-STEP is the distance between any two adjacent keys on the keyboard. Half-steps may be formed in three different ways.

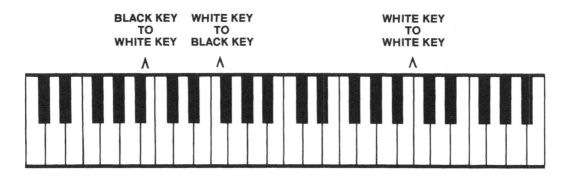

INTRODUCING THE FLAT SIGN (♭)

When a FLAT SIGN appears to the left of a note, lower the note one half-step. In other words, play the first adjacent key to the **left**.

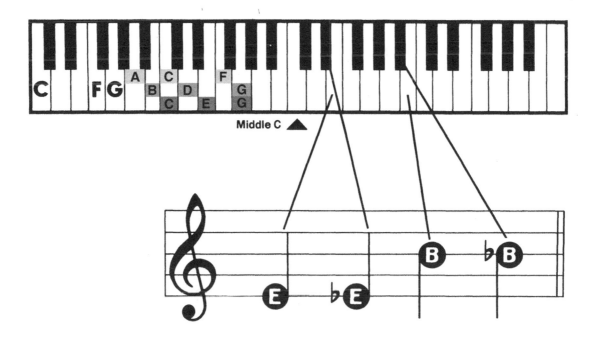

INTRODUCING THE SHARP SIGN (♯)

When a SHARP SIGN appears to the left of any note, raise the note one half-step. In other words, play the first adjacent key to the **right**.

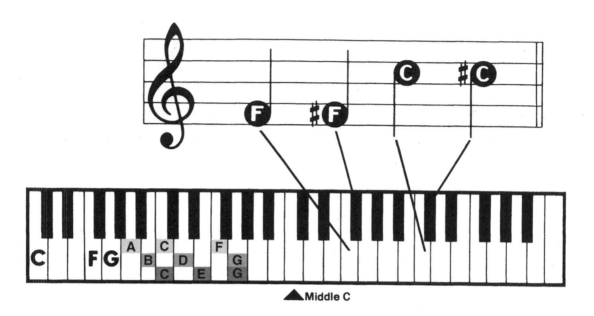

Middle C

NEW NOTES . . . B, C, D and E

Your next song, MY WILD IRISH ROSE, contains four new notes.

● They appear like this on the staff.

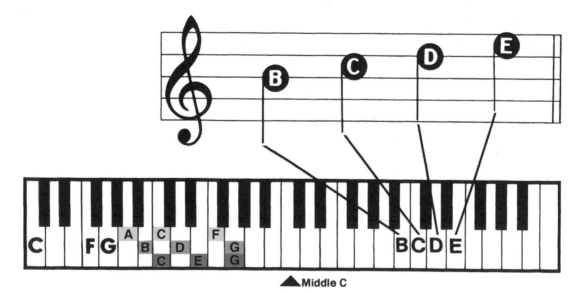

Middle C

● They correspond to these keys on the keyboard.

Song 8 will introduce you to the D7 chord. The B♭ chord is introduced in Song 9. Press these keys and you'll be playing a D7 chord. Be sure you observe the fingering.

Press these keys for a D7 chord.

(C) (D) (F♯)

Fingering: 3 2 1

Middle C

Press these keys and you'll be playing a B♭ chord. Be sure to place the 4th finger on the B♭ note.

Press these keys for a B♭ chord.

(B♭) (D) (F)

Fingering: 4 2 1

Middle C

Song 8: My Wild Irish Rose

Words and Music by
Chauncey Olcott

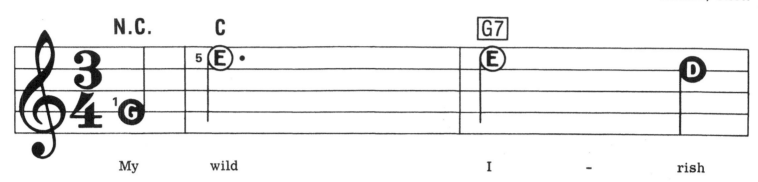

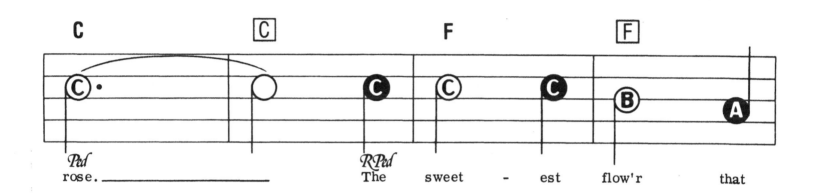

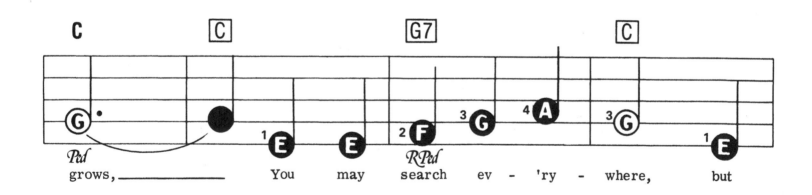

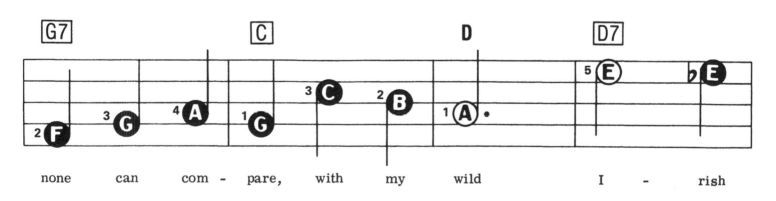

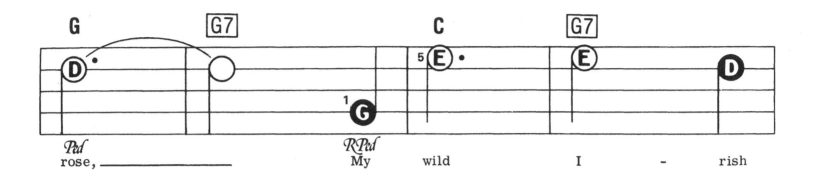

rose, _____ My wild I - rish

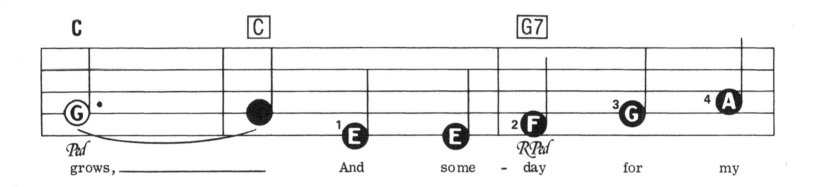

rose _____ The dear - est flow'r that

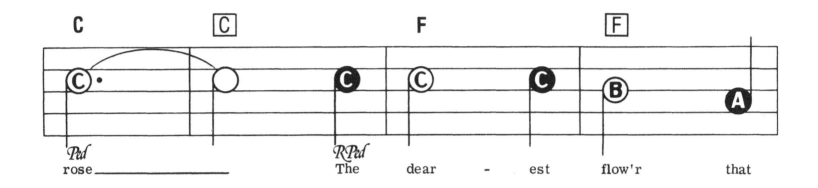

grows, _____ And some - day for my

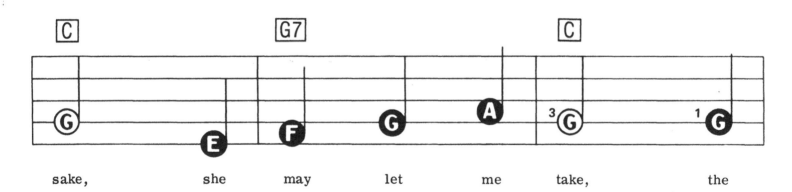

sake, she may let me take, the

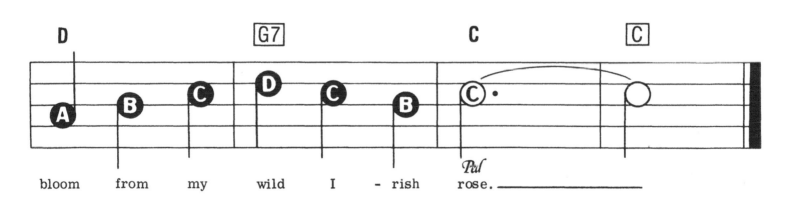

bloom from my wild I - rish rose. _____

Song 9: Sidewalks Of New York

Words and Music by Charles B. Lawlor and
James W. Blake

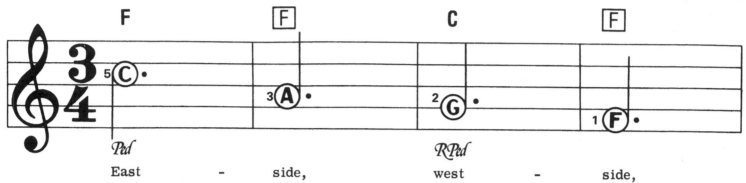

East - side, west - side,

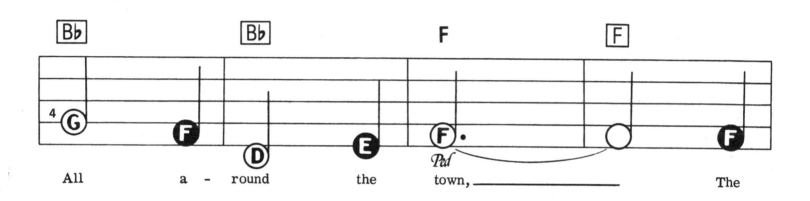

All a - round the town, _____ The

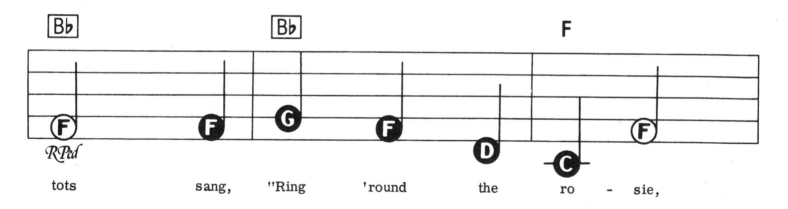

tots sang, "Ring 'round the ro - sie,

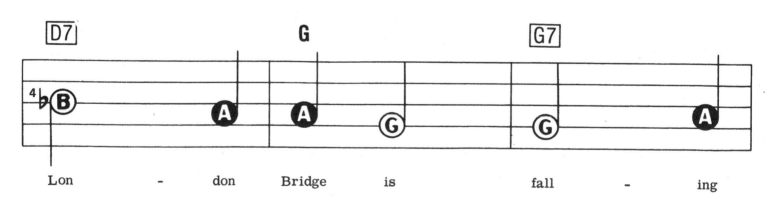

Lon - don Bridge is fall - ing

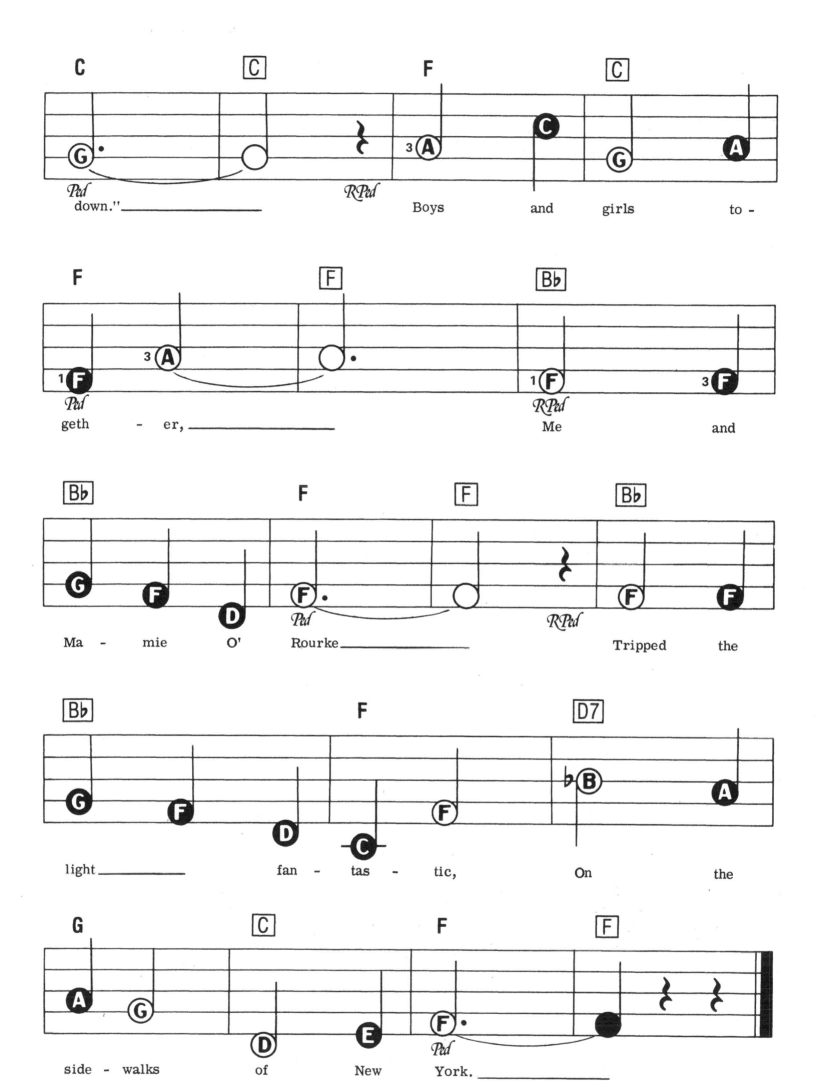

Thus far, each single note that you've played in the accompaniment part has been followed by a left-hand chord. In Song 10, the left-hand part will contain a number of single notes played in succession.

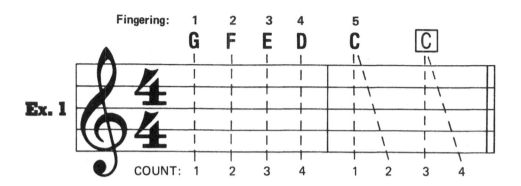

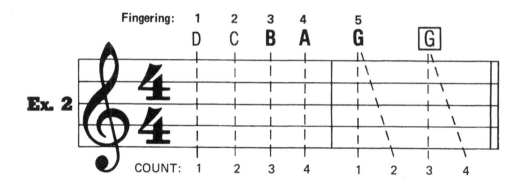

To play Example 1, start by placing the first finger of your left hand (thumb) on the G key.

Use these 5 keys for the single notes in Ex. 1.

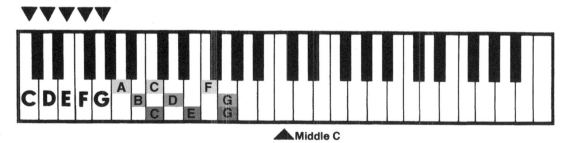

▲ Middle C

To play Example 2, start by placing the first finger of your left hand on the D key.

Use these 5 keys for the single notes in Ex. 2.

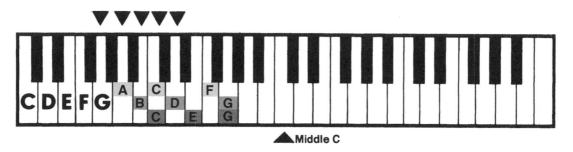

▲Middle C

Try the following exercise before going on. Remember, the number above a letter indicates the finger that should be used to play that single note (the chords are fingered as usual).

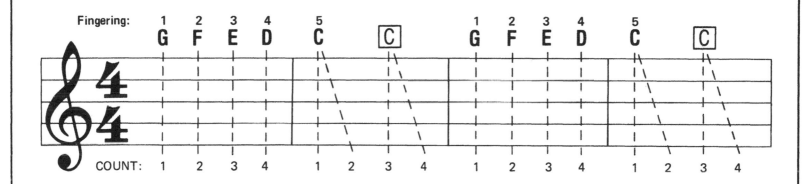

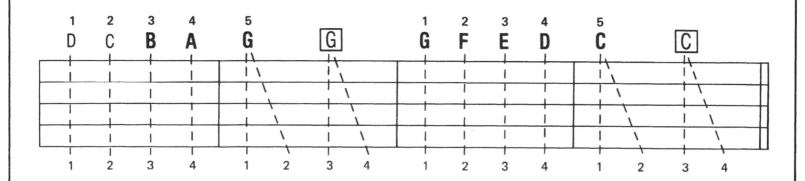

REPEAT SIGNS

REPEAT SIGNS are used in a song when a section of the arrangement or the entire song is to be played again (repeated). Generally, Repeat Signs appear in sets of two.

- There will be one repeat sign (A) at the beginning of the section to be repeated.
- Play up to the repeat sign at the end of this section (B).
- Return to the first repeat sign (A) and play the section again.
- If there is no repeat sign (A), return to the beginning of the song.

1st and 2nd ENDINGS

When two different endings appear within or at the end of a song, here's what to do:

- Play the song up through the first (1) ending.
- Repeat to the closest repeat sign, or back to the beginning.
- Play that section again, skip the first ending (1), but play the second ending (2).

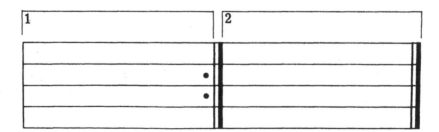

Song 10 contains a new note F.

● It appears like this on the staff.

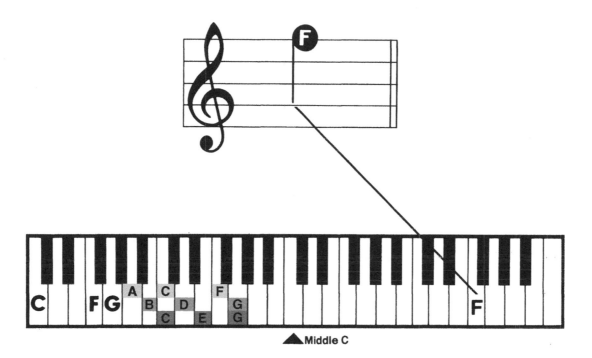

● It corresponds to this key on the keyboard.

29

Song 10: Village Tavern Polka

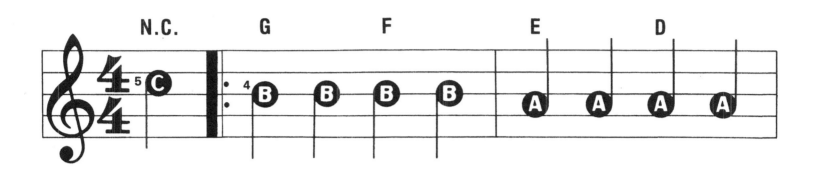

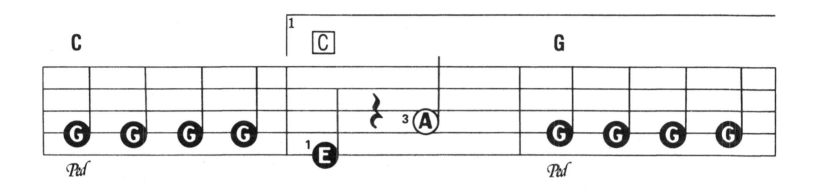

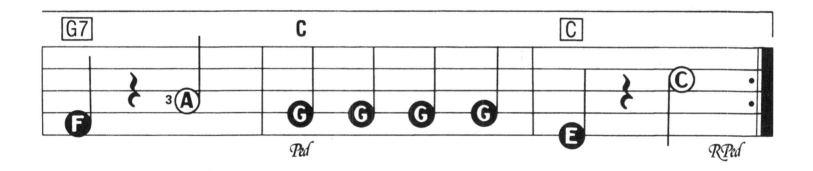

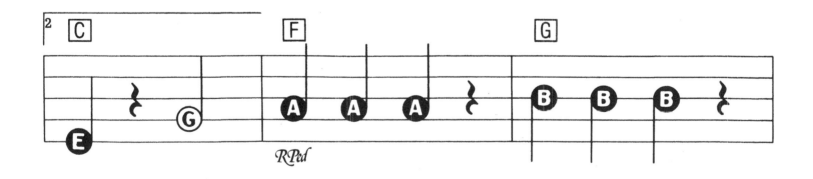

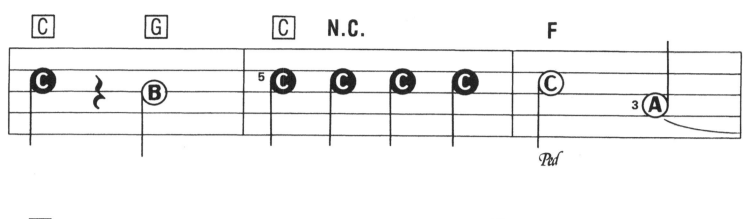

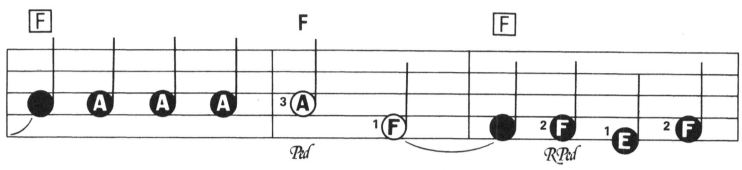

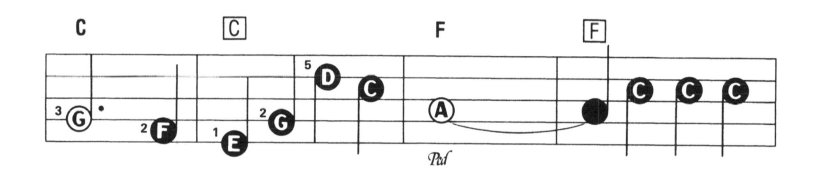

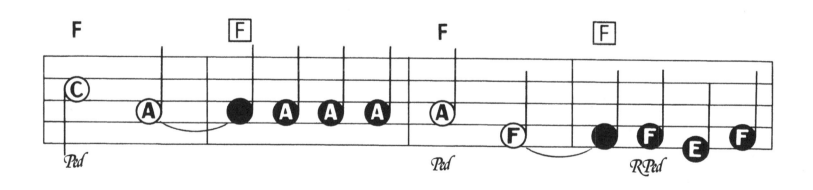

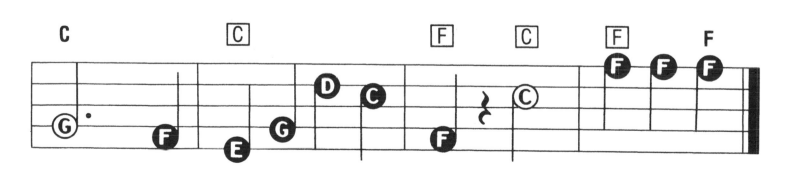

31

● A single eighth note has a flag on its stem, and it receives ½ beat.

½ beat   ½ beat

● Two or more eighth notes are written in a group and connected by a beam.

Two eighth notes equal one full beat   2 beats

● To play and accurately count eighth notes, divide the counting of each beat into 2 parts by saying "and" between each numbered beat.

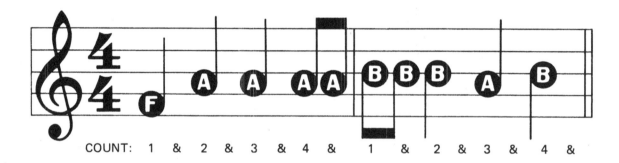

COUNT: 1 & 2 & 3 & 4 &   1 & 2 & 3 & 4 &

INTRODUCING THE EIGHTH REST (ɣ)

The eighth rest receives the same time value as the eighth note.

ɣ = ♪ = ½ beat

32

Song 11: Little Brown Jug

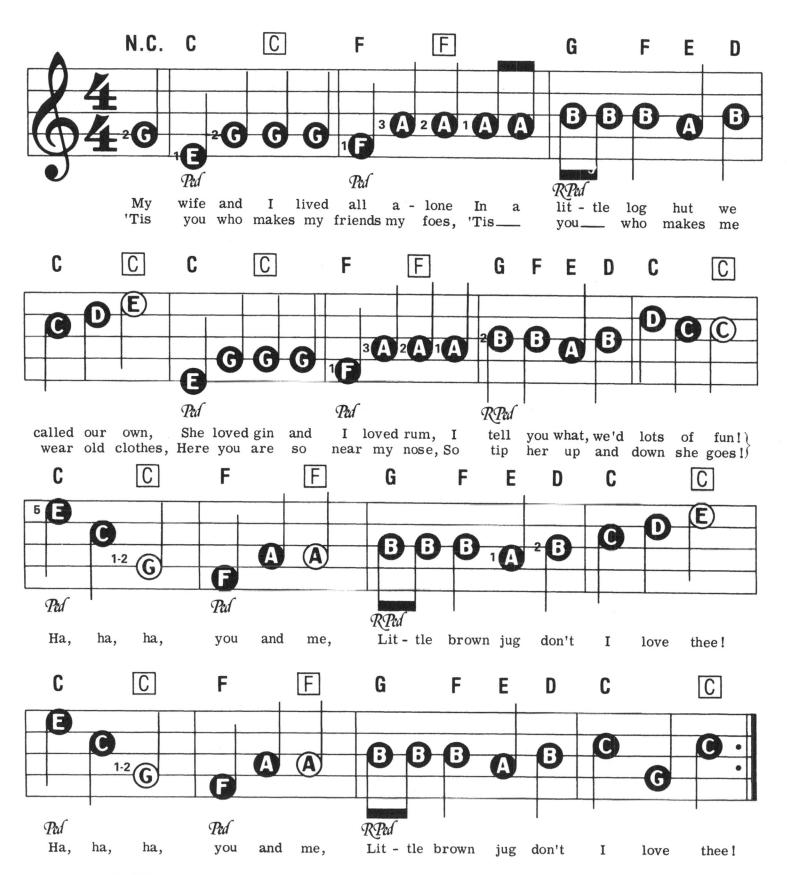

- A dot placed after any note increases that note's value by one half.
- As you learned earlier, the dotted half note receives three beats.

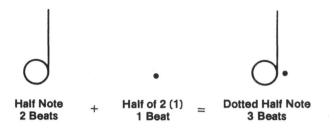

| Half Note | + | Half of 2 (1) | = | Dotted Half Note |
| 2 Beats | | 1 Beat | | 3 Beats |

- The same principle applies to the dotted quarter note.

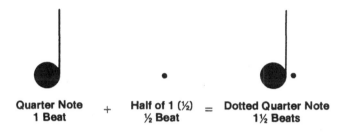

| Quarter Note | + | Half of 1 (½) | = | Dotted Quarter Note |
| 1 Beat | | ½ Beat | | 1½ Beats |

- The dotted quarter note is usually followed by an eighth note.

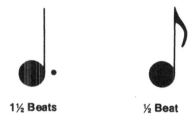

1½ Beats   ½ Beat

Count and play the following exercise before trying Songs 12 and 13.

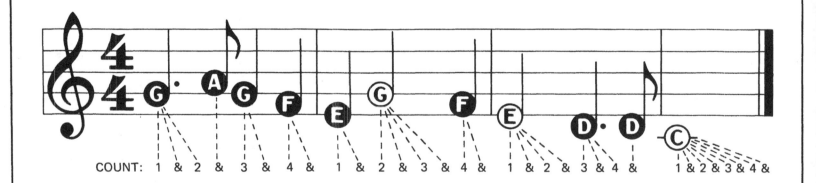

Song 12: She Wore A Yellow Ribbon

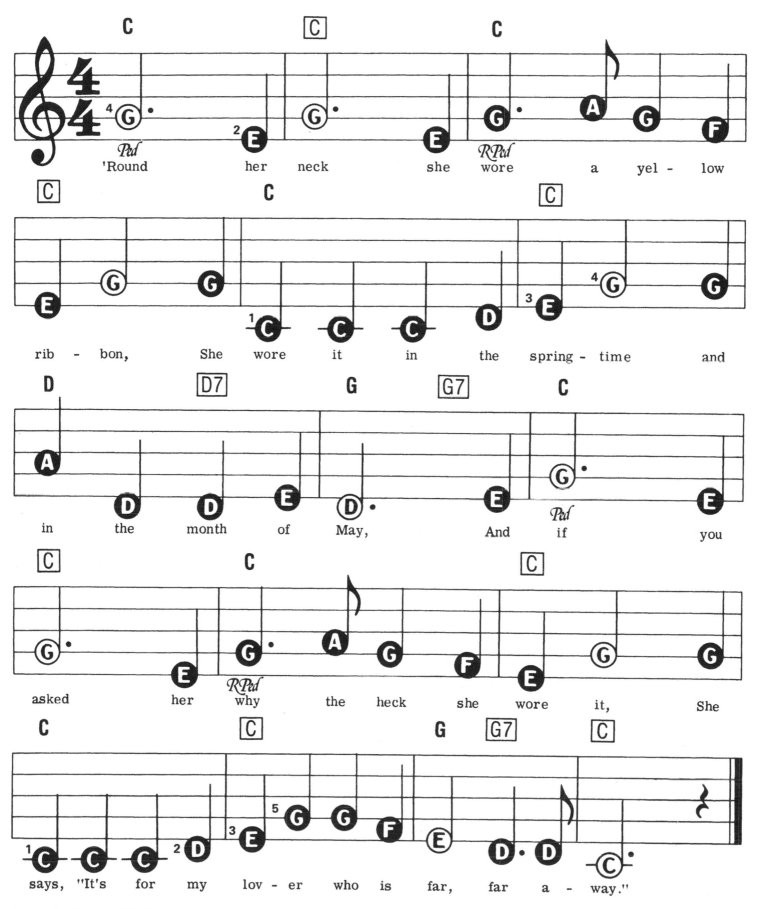

Song 13: Blue Tail Fly

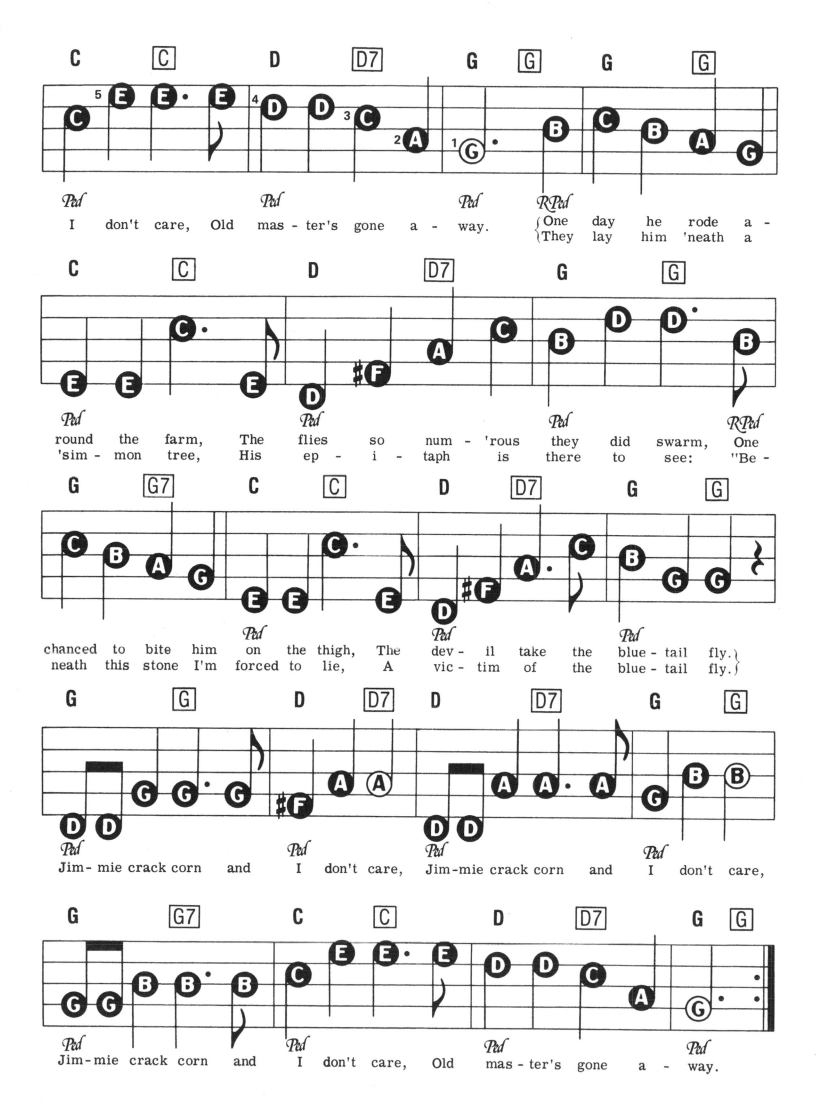

Song 14 will introduce you to two new chords . . . the A minor chord Am (the small m is an abbreviation for minor) and the E chord E. Notice that each chord has two sets of fingering. Try them both; then use the one that feels more comfortable to you.

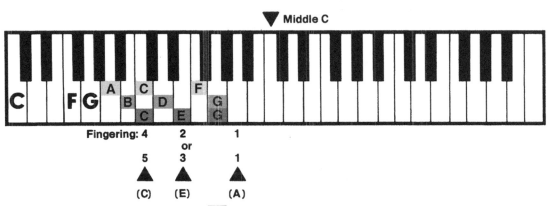

Press these keys for an Am chord.

Press these keys for an 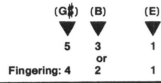 **chord.**

Middle C

Notice that the CAISSONS SONG contains all three accompaniment patterns that you've learned thus far. As a suggestion, it may be wise to try the left-hand part separately a few times before playing both hands together.

Song 14: Caissons Song

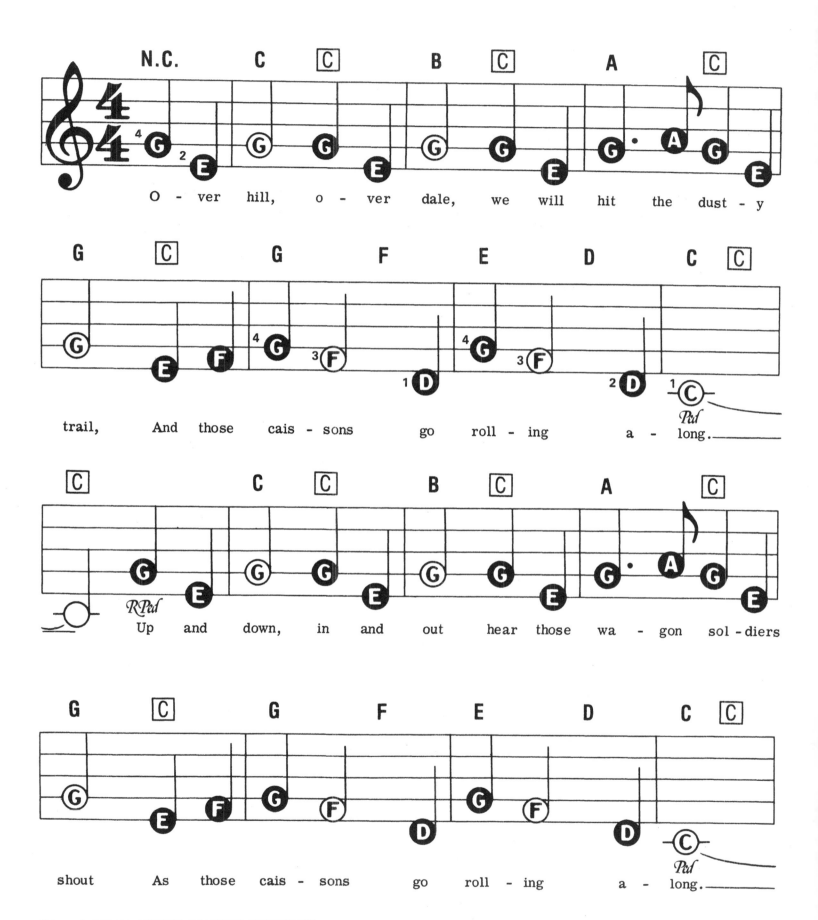

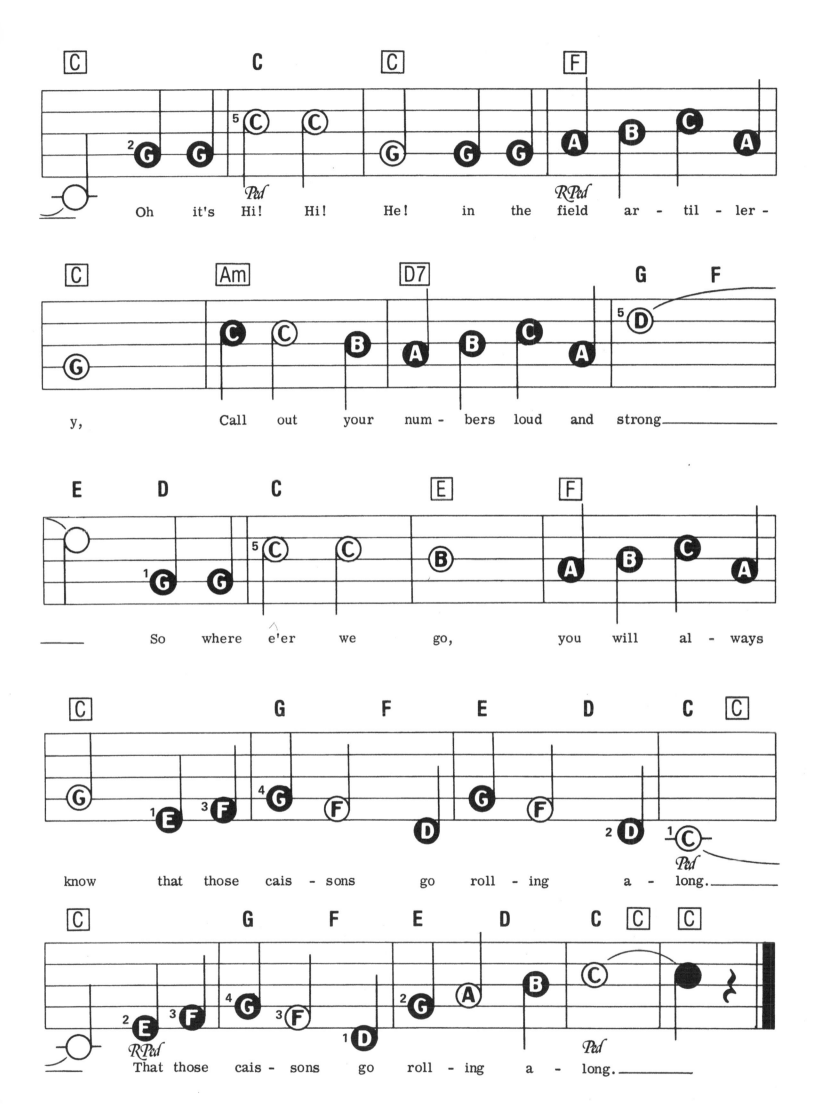

A NEW ACCOMPANIMENT PATTERN ... FOUR BEAT RHYTHM

A new type of accompaniment pattern is introduced in Song 15. This new accompaniment style calls for a chord being struck on each beat in a measure. While the "four-beat" rhythm style is often used in "rock-type" music, it first gained popularity during the 1930's and 1940's. To fully insure a separation of parts and a good balance of sound, play the left-hand chords short and separated (staccato).

D.S. AL CODA

This is another type of repeat sign. Italian in derivation, the letters D.S. are abbreviations for the term "dal segno" which means "from the sign." The entire term means to:

Return to the sign 𝄋 . (See the first line of Song 15.) Then play to this sign ⊕. (See line four of the music.) Then skip to the section marked CODA and play to the end. (See the last line of the music.)

A NEW NOTE ... G

DOWN BY THE RIVERSIDE uses a new G note.

● It appears like this on the staff.

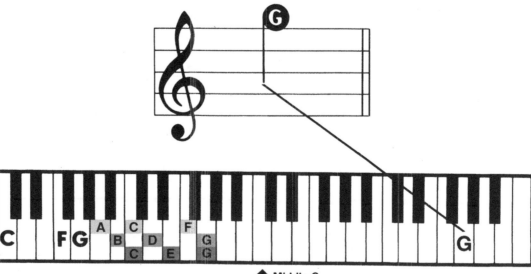

● It corresponds to this key on the keyboard.

You'll need to learn two new chords to complete the last songs in this book. Press these keys and you'll be playing a Dm chord. Again, try both fingerings to determine which feels more comfortable to you.

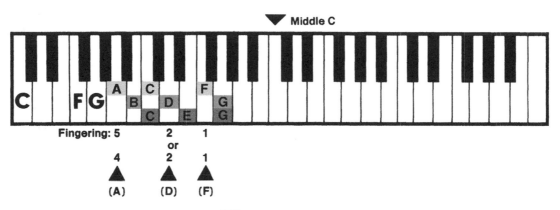

Press these keys for a Dm chord.

The following illustration shows the notes to press to play the new A7 chord. Be sure to watch the fingering carefully.

Press these keys for an A7 chord.

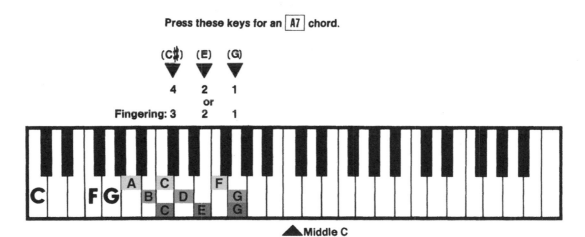

Song 15: Down By The Riverside

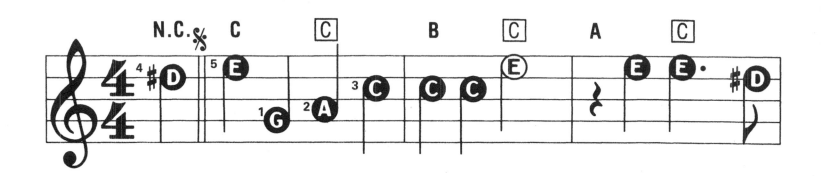

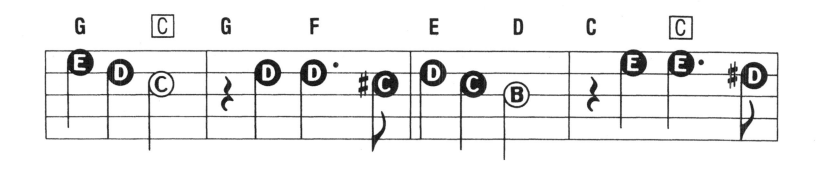

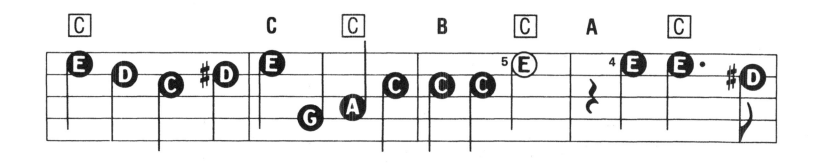

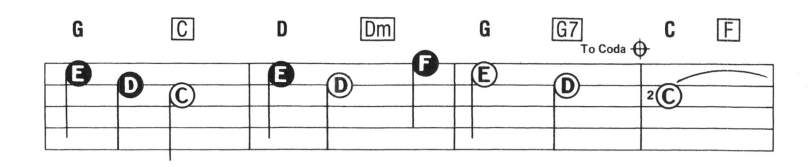

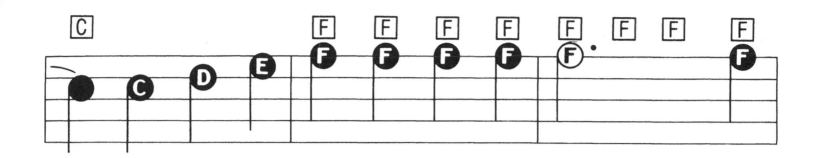

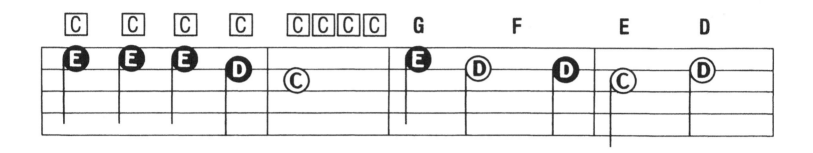

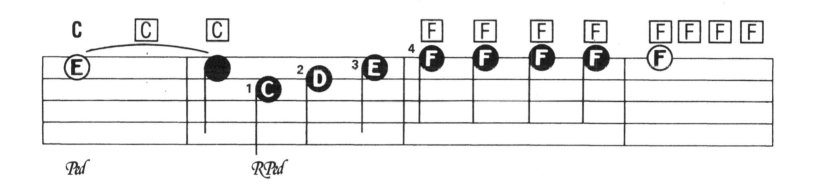

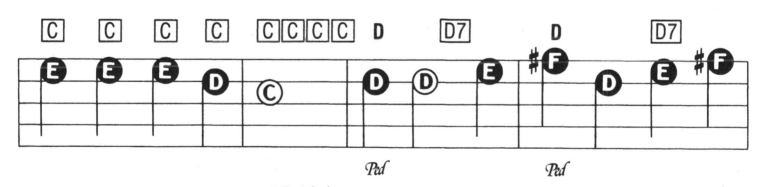

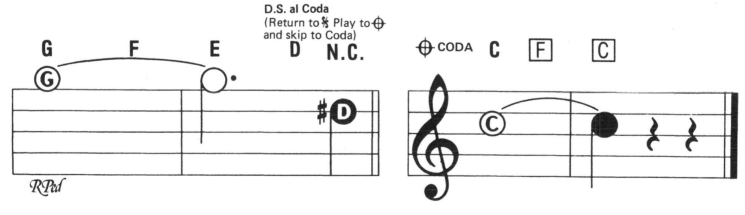

Song 16: Yankee Doodle Dandy

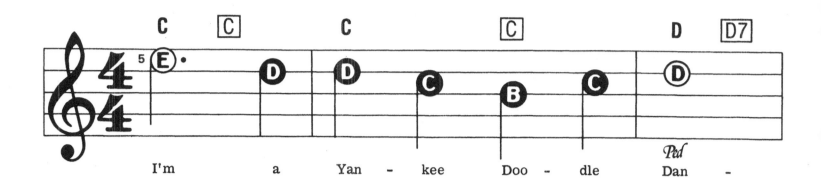

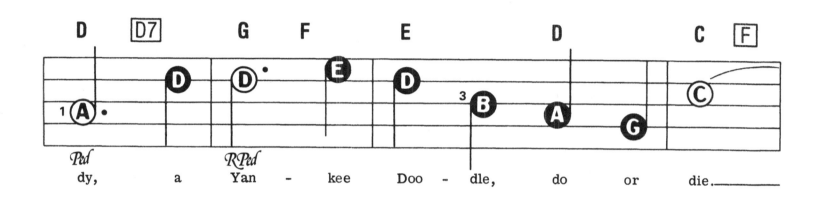

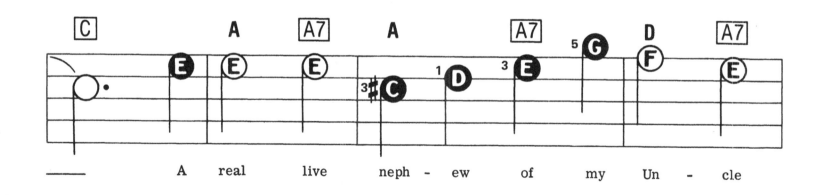

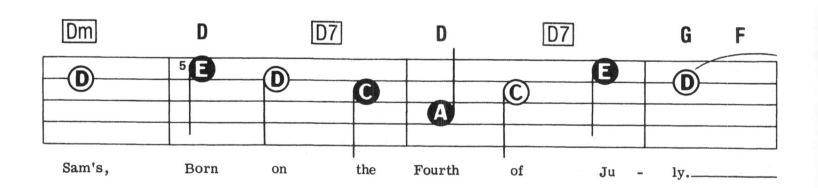

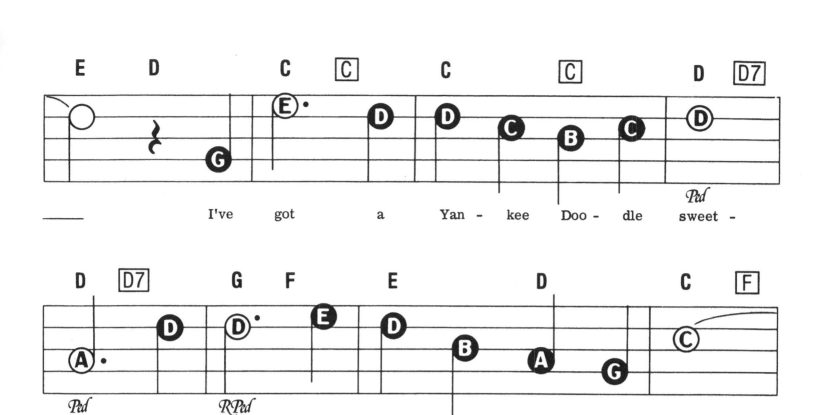

I've got a Yan - kee Doo - dle sweet -

heart, And she's my Yan - kee Doo - dle joy.____

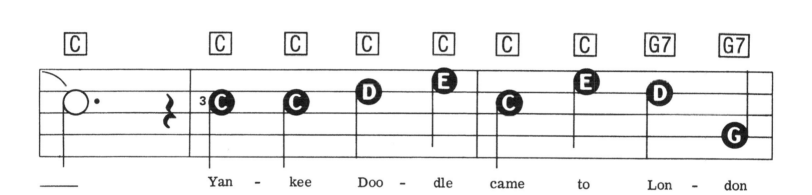

Yan - kee Doo - dle came to Lon - don

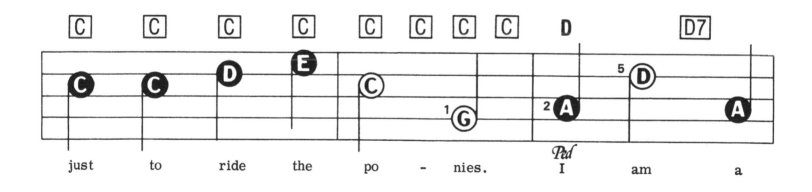

just to ride the po - nies. I am a

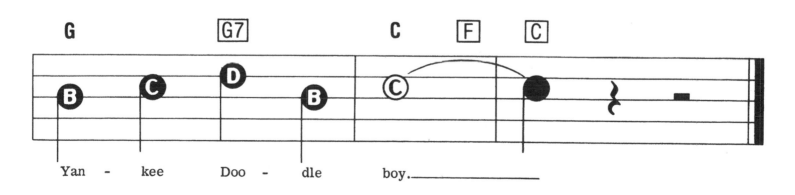

Yan - kee Doo - dle boy.____